101 WALKING JAZZ BASSLINES

Learn to Build & Play Walking Basslines on Every Essential Jazz Chord Sequence

JOHNNY COX

FUNDAMENTAL CHANGES

101 Walking Jazz Bass Lines

Learn to Build & Play Walking Basslines on Every Essential Jazz Chord Sequence

ISBN: 978-1-78933-449-4

Published by **www.fundamental-changes.com**

Copyright © 2024 Johnny Cox

Edited by Joseph Alexander

www.fundamental-changes.com

For over 350 free guitar lessons with videos check out:

www.fundamental-changes.com

Join our free Facebook Community of Cool Musicians

www.facebook.com/groups/fundamentalguitar

Tag us for a share on Instagram: **FundamentalChanges**

Cover Image Copyright: Shutterstock

Contents

Introduction

The term *walking bass* is used to describe basslines made by playing four 1/4 notes in a bar – one note played on each beat to create a feeling of continuous movement. It's a simple idea, but *walking* is a fundamental technique for jazz bass players. A good walking bassline lays a solid foundation for the other musicians in the band.

Jazz is an improvised artform, so most of the time we're not usually playing a bass part that has been written for us – we have to choose the notes we play.

So, how do we choose those notes?

You'll often hear jazz bass players talk about *spelling out the harmony* with their basslines. In simple terms, this means following the chord progression and using the notes that make up each chord, arranged in different ways to form a walking bassline.

So, the first thing we need to know before we create a walking line is, what are the chords?

In this book, I'm going to show you how I created 101 jazz walking basslines on some of the most important chord progressions in jazz. Along the way, I'll explain the techniques I used to keep things interesting, so that you can instantly add these ideas to your playing.

By the time you've finished this book, you'll not only know dozens of walking bass ideas that you can play on any jazz tune, you'll also have the skills to compose your own walking lines on any chord progression in real time.

There is a huge amount of freedom and creativity in the construction and improvisation of walking basslines, so I think you're going to really enjoy working through this book. By the end, you'll be a much better musician.

Have fun!

Johnny

Get the Audio

The audio files for this book are available to download for free from **www.fundamental-changes.com.** The link is in the top right-hand corner. Click on the "Bass" link then simply select this book title from the drop-down menu and follow the instructions to get the audio.

We recommend that you download the files directly to your computer, not to your tablet, and extract them there before adding them to your media library.

For over 350 free guitar lessons with videos check out:

www.fundamental-changes.com

Join our free Facebook Community of Cool Musicians

www.facebook.com/groups/fundamentalguitar

Tag us for a share on Instagram: **FundamentalChanges**

Chapter One – Major II–V–I

The ii–V–I (pronounced two five one) sequence is the most common chord progression in jazz, so learning musical ways to navigate it is a fundamental part of learning walking bass.

If you've never heard the term before, here's a quick explanation of what it means. Feel free to skip ahead if you're already on top of your jazz theory game!

The C Major scale contains the notes: C D E F G A B

The chords in the key of C Major are built by grouping notes in 3rds – essentially "stacking" alternate notes of the scale.

If we start on the note C (the root of the chord), then add three notes, each one a 3rd above the last, we get this pattern:

C D **E** F **G** A **B**

The bold notes, C E G B, create the chord CMaj7.

If we move to the second note of the scale, D, and repeat the process, we get D F A C, which spells Dmin7, etc.

This process is called harmonisation, and if we harmonise the entire scale, we build the sequence of chords shown in the table below.

The *quality* of the chords (i.e., whether they are major or minor) is always the same when you harmonise any major scale. So, the ii chord, for example, is *always* a minor 7th. In the key of C Major, it's a Dm7. If we were in the key of D Major, it would be an Em7, etc.

In the table below, you'll notice that each note and chord in the scale is assigned a Roman numeral. These Roman numerals are used by jazz musicians as a shorthand method for referring to a chord sequence. For example, they might scribble down ii–V–I in the key of C, which would mean playing Dm7 – G7 – Cmaj7.

C	D	E	F	G	A	B
I	ii	iii	IV	V	iv	vii
CMaj7	Dm7	Em7	FMaj7	G7	Am7	Bm7b5
C E G B	D F A C	E G B D	F A C E	G B D F	A C E G	B D F A

Now, listen to and play Example 1a, which is played over the chords Dm7 – G7 – Cmaj7.

To create this example, I used this simple strategy:

1. On each chord, first play the root note.

2. Play the 3rd on the second beat.

3. Play the 5th on the third beat.

4. Then play either the 3rd or the root on the fourth beat.

Here are the chord tones I used, illustrated in a table.

Chord	Root	3rd	5th
Dm7 (ii)	D	F	A
G7 (V)	G	B	D
CMaj (I)	C	E	G

Example 1a:

Here's another example using the same idea.

Example 1b:

These lines are simple to create when we know our chord tones. Bass players must practice playing chord tones in the same way that guitar players practice playing chords.

In rock and pop, it's common to hear basslines that use root and 5th interval patterns, but in jazz, 3rds are used more often because they help to identify whether the chord is major or minor, and this assists the bass player in outlining the harmony.

Refer back to the table above and play just the root and 3rd of each of the chords. With just this tiny bit of harmonic information, we can hear that it spells one chord that has a minor 3rd (a distance of three frets on the bass) and two chords that have a major 3rd (a distance of four frets).

Practice Tip

Practice locating the 3rds on your bass for each chord in the key of C Major. Play a major 3rd for every major chord type (Cmaj7, Fmaj7, G7), and a minor 3rd for every minor chord type (Dm7, Em7, Am7, Bm7b5).

There are obviously 3rds above the pitch of the root note, but we can also find 3rds below them too. The following exercise moves through each chord, first playing 3rds above the root notes, then below.

Example 1c:

Now let's use this idea musically. It sounds great to start on a root note then drop to a 3rd pitched below that root note.

Example 1d:

You can vary your lines by playing the 3rd before you play the root.

Having the 3rd as the first note creates an *inversion*. This is when the bass note is not the root note of the chord, but one of the other notes, like the 3rd or the 5th.

In rock/pop, inversions are sometimes called slash chords because they're written like this: C/E. We don't usually play inversions in a pop song unless a slash chord is specifically written. But, in jazz, we can use inversions in our lines almost whenever we like.

This is what it sounds like.

Example 1e:

7ths are also important intervals in jazz. Just like 3rds, 7ths can be major or minor. However, a minor 7th doesn't necessarily mean a chord is minor. The chord G7 (the V chord) has a major 3rd and a minor 7th.

Here's an exercise for playing roots and 7ths in the key of C Major. First ascending from root to 7th and then descending to the 7th.

Example 1f:

Here's a walking bassline built on roots and 7ths.

Example 1g:

The following examples combine everything we've looked at so far: roots, 3rds, 5ths, 7ths and inversions.

Example 1h:

Example 1i:

It can be effective to incorporate larger interval jumps into our walking basslines, as seen between the last two notes of Example 1j. I've moved from the 5th of the C major chord (G) to the 3rd (E).

Instead of moving to the E in the same octave as G, I've dropped a whole octave down to the open string. Using an open string in this way not only creates a dramatic interval leap, it's also helpful in giving us time to change position on the fretboard.

Example 1j:

Practice Tip

When practicing arpeggios or chord tones, think about which notes in the chord can be played on open strings. When you play an open string, use it as an opportunity to shift position on the fretboard and make your lines sound smoother.

Example 1k:

Another variation of this idea is to change the order of the notes. For example, instead of playing root, 3rd, 5th, 7th, we could play root, 5th, 3rd, 7th.

Example 1k1:

You can do this exercise starting on different notes in the chord. This example starts on the 3rd.

Example 1k2:

And here's one that begins each bar on the 5th.

Example 1k3:

Here are a few more examples that I've created with these kinds of patterns on a Major ii–V–I in C. They are longer examples and I've doubled the number of beats on each chord.

Example 1l:

Example 1m:

Let's recap:

1. Chord tones are the strongest notes we can use to spell out the harmony with our walking basslines.

2. Roots and 3rds are particularly strong notes, and we can also target 7ths and 5ths.

However, a good jazz walking bassline usually doesn't use only chord tones, and the next important topic to address is "passing notes".

Passing notes can come from one of two sources:

1. Scale tones – meaning any other note from the key i.e. the 2nd, 4th, or 6th.

2. Chromatic notes – meaning any note that is *not* in the key.

Let's explore an example that uses scale tones as passing notes. In Example 1n I've used the following strategy:

1. Play a chord tone (root, 3rd, 5th or 7th) on beats 1 and 3. These are the *target* notes.

2. Play a scale tone (2nd, 4th, 6th) on beats 2 and 4. These are the *passing* notes.

Example 1n:

The longer a chord lasts, the more you need to use passing notes to keep the bassline engaging.

For example, if you only have two beats on a chord, you can easily create a bassline using just the root and 3rd. However, if the same chord extends over eight beats, it's crucial to play additional notes.

We'll play that progression again, but this time we'll also use other notes from the scale as passing notes. This approach allows for a richer, more varied bassline that keeps the listener's interest over longer chord durations.

Example 1o:

This system, in its simplest form, is:

1. Play a chord tone on beats 1 and 3.

2. Play any note from the scale on beats 2 and 4.

Here are two more examples.

Example 1p:

Example 1q:

We can also use chromatic notes to spice up our basslines. A chromatic note is any note that isn't in the key.

In the key of C Major (C D E F G A B) that simply means any note which has a sharp or flat, for example C# or Gb.

Chromatics can be used as passing notes on beats 2 and 4.

The easiest way to add chromatic notes to our basslines is to play a chromatic *approach* note i.e., one fret *above* or *below* the target note.

Here is my strategy for the following example:

1. Play a chord tone on beats 1 and 3 (*target notes*).

2. Play a note one fret above or below a target note on beats 2 and 4 (*chromatic notes*).

Example 1r:

Practice Tip

A good way to practice adding chromatic notes is to play arpeggios that have chromatic approach notes placed in between every note of the chord.

The first two bars of the following exercise show how to add chromatic approach notes one fret *below* the chord tones, and bars 3-4 feature chromatic approach notes added one fret *above* each chord tone.

Example 1s:

Good walking basslines combine the ideas we've explored in this chapter into logical, flowing and (ideally) non-repetitive lines.

So, the final strategy for this chapter is:

1. Play a chord tone on beats 1 and 3 (root, 3rd, 5th or 7th).

2. Play a passing note on beats 2 and 4 (which can be any note from the key or a chromatic approach note).

Example 1t:

Example 1u:

Practice jamming along to a Major ii–V–i backing track (there are plenty of free ones available online) and go back over the strategies we've used in this chapter before moving on.

Chapter Two – Minor II–V–I

In Chapter One we looked at walking bass ideas we can play in major keys, but ii–V–i progressions are fundamental in minor keys too.

Where the major ii–V–I looked like this:

Dm7 – G7 – Cmaj7

The minor ii–V–i looks like this:

Dm7b5 – G7 – Cm6

We'll discuss the difference in the ii chord in a moment, but the fundamental difference in the progression is the i chord, which is now minor rather than major. As you know, a C major chord contains the notes C E G, whereas a C minor chord comprises the notes C Eb G. So, we just need to flatten the 3rd (E to Eb) to walk on this minor chord using chord tones.

However, there is another common change to the i chord in the minor ii–V–i that you need to know about.

Over the Major ii–V–I we used the major scale as the main source of our note choices. In jazz, it's common to use the Melodic Minor scale when playing in minor keys.

The melodic minor differs from the Major scale by just one note – the flattened 3rd – every other note is the same. This means that you only need to make one small adjustment to a scale you already know.

This subtle shift significantly alters the mood and possibilities of the harmony, and provides a different foundation for improvisation and melody.

C Major: C D E F G A B C

C Melodic Minor: C D Eb F G A B C

If you're familiar with the Melodic Minor scale from any classical music studies, it's important to know that jazz musicians use this scale a bit differently. In jazz, the Melodic Minor scale is played the same way both ascending and descending (unlike in classical music, where the scale changes on its descent).

In a jazz ii–V–i we typically don't play Cm7 for the i chord because it has a b7 (Bb) and, as you can see above, the Melodic Minor has a natural 7th (B).

To accommodate this note, it's common to play a C minor 6 for the i chord, which has the notes C Eb G A, with the 6th degree of the Melodic Minor scale replacing the 7th. This adaptation provides the distinct sound that is characteristic of jazz minor tunes. Here is how it sounds:

Example 2a:

The dominant V chord is treated the same way in both major and minor keys, but something different also happens on the ii chord in minor progressions.

As well as playing a minor 6 for chord i, in jazz minor tunes it's common to play a minor 7b5 (or half-diminished) for chord ii.

Let's look at the implications of this change.

The C Melodic Minor scale includes the notes D F A C, which match the chord tones of Dm7. But rather than play a straight Dm7 chord, in jazz you'll see this changed into Dm7b5 by flattening the 5th (A to Ab).

The reasons for this are a little complicated, but essentially the minor 7b5 chord is "borrowed" from the Harmonic Minor scale in order to spice up the harmony and give soloists more interesting chords to improvise over.

The C Harmonic Minor scale has the notes C D Eb F G Ab B C, so, you might wonder, "Why not just use the harmonic minor for playing over each of these chords?"

That is definitely an option, but this kind of sound is much more suited to Gypsy Jazz and can sound a little old fashioned in a modern jazz context.

The chord tones for the ii chord are D F Ab C, to form D half-diminished or Dm7b5. This is the correct chord to use for the ii chord in a minor key progression in a modern jazz context.

Example 2b:

We can summarise this theory by saying there are just two new rules we must remember for playing chord tones on a minor ii–V–i:

1. Flatten the 5th of the ii chord.

2. Flatten the 3rd of the i chord.

The following examples show three ways of negotiating these chord changes, focusing on different chord tones.

Example 2c:

Example 2d:

Example 2e:

Now, here are some longer form examples that use only chord tones.

Example 2f:

Example 2g:

Now let's apply the same bassline building principles we used in Chapter One. Here, we introduce some passing notes from the C Melodic Minor scale.

Example 2h:

Example 2i:

These next examples use chromatic passing notes and approach notes.

Example 2j:

Example 2k:

To learn jazz, it's essential to understand the ii–V–I, and we've looked at how to play it in both major and minor keys. We've also played it in both short (two bars) and long (four bars) forms.

But major and minor ii–V–Is crop up in virtually every jazz standard tune in a variety of keys, so before we move on, let's play some examples in different keys.

When we change to a new key, one thing that immediately becomes apparent is that we must know where all of our chord tones are located!

This is an example in the key of G Major.

Example 2l:

Here is a ii-V-I in the key of Bb Major.

Example 2m:

This example is in the key of D Minor.

Example 2n:

Here's another minor key example, this time in F Minor.

Example 2o:

Practice Tip

To improvise lines like these, we must know the scale for the key as well as the relevant chord tones. For example, this minor ii–V–i uses the notes of the A Melodic Minor scale as passing notes to connect the chord tones.

Example 2p:

Jazz standards often feature ii–V–Is in multiple keys during the same song, so the following example features two major key ii–V–Is: first in Bb Major then Ab Major.

Example 2q:

Many jazz tunes, such as the ever-popular *Autumn Leaves*, combine major and minor ii–V–Is in their structure.

Example 2r features a major ii–V–I in A Major and a minor ii–V–i in F# Minor. They have the same key signature, so we call these *relative keys*.

Example 2r:

To continue working on your ii–V–I walking basslines, I suggest the following plan of action:

1. Find a nice, medium-paced jazz drum loop to practice to.

2. Imagine a progression that combines a minor and major ii–V–I, or better still get a pianist or guitarist friend to lay down some chords for you. Start with Am7 – D7 – Gmaj7, followed by F#m7b5 – B7 – Em6.

3. First, make sure you know the location of all the chord tones for each chord in the sequence and practice moving between them on the fretboard.

4. Now put on the loop and play through the changes using only chord tones.

5. Next, make sure you know the G Major scale and the E Melodic Minor scale – both of which you'll draw from to add passing scale notes.

6. Put on the loop and play through the changes again, this time adding passing scale tones and finding as many different pathways through the chords as you can.

7. Finally, experiment with chromatic passing notes to make your bassline more exciting.

Chapter Three – Rhythm Changes I–VI–II–V

The I–VI–ii–V progression is a common jazz turnaround that is typically played at the end of a section to guide us seamlessly into the next part, or played at the end of a tune.

One of the most iconic ways in which this sequence has been used is known as the Rhythm Changes, from George Gershwin's classic *I Got Rhythm*. This 32-bar progression has been used as the basis for many well-known jazz standards, including Sonny Rollins' *Oleo* and Charlie Parker's *Anthropology*, to name just two.

It's an essential slice of jazz harmony that you need to know how to play walking bass over, so this chapter is dedicated to tackling it.

Rhythm Changes are very often played in the key of Bb Major. Let's begin by examining the diatonic seventh chords that belong to this key to understand how they fit into the progression.

Bb	C	D	Eb	F	G	A
I	ii	iii	IV	V	vi	vii
BbMaj7	Cm7	Dm7	EbMaj7	F7	Gm7	Am7b5
Bb D F A	C Eb G Bb	D F A C	Eb G Bb D	F A C Eb	G Bb D F	A C Eb G

If we stuck exactly to the diatonic chords in the key, the Rhythm Changes progression would be,

BbMaj7 – Gm7 – Cm7 – F7

But it is frequently written as,

BbMaj7 – G7 – Cm7 – F7

Jazz musicians often change the quality of a minor chord to make it dominant. The simple reason for doing so here is that G7 wants to resolve to Cm7 more strongly than Gm7.

So, rather than playing Gm7 (G Bb D F) we'll use G7 (G B D F). Here, G7 is functioning as the V chord of C minor. This modification changes only one note in the VI chord: Bb becomes B natural.

Aside from this detail, the approaches we'll take to walking on the I, ii and V chords will be the same as they were for the major key progressions we've already explored.

Let's begin by playing roots and 3rds to construct a bassline over this progression.

Example 3a:

Example 3b:

We can add 5ths and 7ths too.

Example 3c:

Example 3d:

A common chord substitution used in Rhythm Changes is to play chord iii (Dm7) in place of chord I (BbMaj7).

This idea works because Dm7 and BbMaj7 both contain the notes D, F and A. In fact, if a bass player plays the note Bb under a Dm7 chord, the sound that chord makes becomes Bbmaj9. The point is, *thinking* Dm7 instead of BbMaj7 opens up a new perspective for creating interesting basslines.

Example 3e:

The chord progression iii–VI–ii–V is known as a Cycle of Fifths sequence. In other words, the distance between the notes D and G is a 5th interval; G to C is a 5th; C to F is a 5th, and so is F to Bb.

Example 3f:

The progressions I–VI–ii–V and iii–VI–ii–V are often used interchangeably. Here's how it might be played:

Example 3g:

With only two beats on each chord, it works well to create lines with the root note and one other chord tone on each chord, like this.

Example 3h:

Now let's try a different approach using chromatic approach notes. The formula for the following example is as follows:

1. Play the root note on the first beat of every new chord.

2. Then, on the next beat, play a note that is one fret (a half-step or semitone) either side of the subsequent root note.

Example 3i:

Here are some more examples that combine all the ideas we've covered in this chapter.

Example 3j:

Example 3k:

Example 3l:

There are many variations of *minor key* turnarounds, but I–VI–ii–V works well and can be used in minor key standards like *Softly as In a Morning Sunrise*.

The i, ii and V chords are the same as the minor ii–V–i examples in Chapter 2. In the key of Bb Minor, that would give us the chords Bbm6, Cm7b5 and F7.

This is our scale:

Bb Melodic Minor

Bb	C	Db	Eb	F	G	A
R	2nd	3rd	4th	5th	6th	7th

The sixth note in the scale is G, and if we harmonise it, we get the notes G Bb Db F, which makes a Gm7b5 chord. So, we'll play both the ii and the vi chords as half diminished (minor 7b5).

Example 3m:

Example 3n:

Examine the i and vi chords more closely and you'll see that they contain the same notes: Bb, Db, F and G.

In fact, the only distinction between Bbm6 and Gm7b5 is which note is played as the root.

These two chords are inversions of each other and playing different bass notes gives us the opportunity to influence the harmony, since the bass note we choose dictates the perceived chord.

When a pianist or guitarist plays those four notes, if the bass plays a Bb, the chord sounds like Bbm6. If we play a G, it becomes Gm7b5.

This concept can be applied to the jazz standard, *Softly, as in a Morning Sunrise*. Typically, the first four bars of this standard are written in the key of C Minor as follows:

Example 3o:

Example 3o only uses the i, ii and V chords, but if we play the root note of chord vi on beat three in bars 1 and 3, then the progression becomes i–vi–ii–V.

Example 3p:

Example 3q:

Another minor key standard that starts with the same progression is *Yesterdays*, which is often played in the key of D Minor.

Example 3r:

Now that you're beginning to find your way around the I–VI–ii–V progression, follow the practice strategy laid out at the end of Chapter Two. Put together a practice loop and apply the different bassline building approaches you've learned. Also practice the sequence in lots of different keys!

Chapter Four – The Rhythm Changes Middle Eight

In the previous chapter, we explored the I–VI–ii–V progression of the Rhythm Changes and its common substitution the iii–VI–ii–V, which naturally follows the Cycle of Fifths.

We saw that in the key of Bb Major, iii–VI–ii–V is Dm7 – G7 – Cm7 – F7.

We noted that the VI chord (normally Gm7 in the key of Bb Major) is changed to G7 to spice up the harmony. Well, what if we changed *every chord* in that sequence to be a dominant chord, so that we ended up with D7 – G7 – C7 – F7?

This is exactly what happens in the bridge or middle-eight of the Rhythm Changes sequence.

Example 4a

This change means that the iii chord now acts as the dominant V of the VI chord, which leads to the dominant V of the ii chord, which becomes the dominant V chord of the actual V chord of the key. It creates a seamless dominant Cycle of 5ths.

This dominant cycle can also work as a turnaround, much like the conventional iii–VI–ii–V progression. It adds a strong sense of movement and resolution back to the start of the cycle or onward in the progression.

Example 4b

The use of a dominant cycle in the middle-eight of the Rhythm Changes highlights how this progression can anchor a key part of a song, giving it a distinct flavour that's easy to recognize, and effective in driving the harmony forward.

Let's walk on this sequence using only chord tones.

Example 4c:

The longer form, with two bars on each chord, provides a great opportunity to explore different walking bass strategies using scales, passing notes and approach notes.

Example 4d uses a simple formula:

1. The first bar of each chord uses chord tones.

2. The second bar of each chord uses a simple descending scale pattern: root 7th, 6th, 5th.

The descending pattern falls nicely onto the next root note of each chord change.

Example 4d:

The next example takes the idea of using scale tones a step further. The scale that perfectly fits a dominant 7 chord is the Mixolydian. The Mixolydian is identical to the Major scale except it has a flattened 7th, so its scale formula is: 1 2 3 4 5 6 b7.

In order to navigate this chord progression, we must use a different Mixolydian scale for each chord. Example 4e uses D Mixolydian for the D7 chord, G Mixolydian for the G7 chord, etc.

Here are the notes for each scale.

D Mixolydian

D	E	F#	G	A	B	C
R	2nd	3rd	4th	5th	6th	b7th

G Mixolydian

G	A	B	C	D	E	F
R	2nd	3rd	4th	5th	6th	b7th

C Mixolydian

C	D	E	F	G	A	Bb
R	2nd	3rd	4th	5th	6th	b7th

F Mixolydian

F	G	A	Bb	C	D	Eb
R	2nd	3rd	4th	5th	6th	b7th

So, we can think of each chord as being its own separate key with its own scale.

Although the line below is built around scales, I've arranged it so that we're mostly playing chord tones on the strong beats of the bar.

Example 4e:

Being able to place the chord tones where we want is crucial for creating scale-based walking basslines that groove.

Here's another example that follows the same concept.

Example 4f:

Placing chord tones on the strong beats while improvising a walking bass line isn't always easy, so adding chromatic passing notes or approach notes is incredibly helpful in ensuring chord tones fall on the beats.

For instance, if you're playing a scale line similar to examples 4e and 4f, and you find yourself approaching a chord tone on beat 2 or 4, you can add a chromatic note just before the chord tone.

This technique ensures that your walking basslines maintain a rhythmic and harmonic clarity. Here are two examples.

Example 4g:

Example 4h:

Here's another idea that uses chromatic approach notes.

1. Play chord tones on beats 1 and 3.

2. Play a chromatic approach note on beats 2 and 4.

Example 4i:

Here are some examples that combine all the different elements and strategies we've looked at so far.

Example 4j:

Example 4k:

Example 4l:

Another common approach when playing the Rhythm Changes middle-eight is to change all four dominant chords into ii–V progressions. This idea works because the movement from ii to V is so fundamental in jazz that we often add the ii chord before a dominant chord, even if it isn't written on the chord chart.

For example, if a dominant chord lasts for one bar, we can split it by playing two beats of the ii chord and two beats of the V chord. If the dominant chord extends over two bars, which is what we see here, then you can play the ii chord for one bar and the V chord for the next bar.

Earlier, I mentioned thinking of each chord in the middle eight as its own scale or key, and here we're simply extending that idea, treating the progression as ii–Vs in four key centres.

For example, in bars 1-2, we view D7 as the V chord in the key of G Major, and precede it with its ii chord from that key, Am7.

In bars 3-4, we view G7 as the V chord in C Major, and precede it with its ii chord (Dm7), and so on.

Following this approach, the progression is outlined by these ii–V pairings.

Example 4m:

Here's another example that uses the same idea.

Example 4n:

Rhythm Changes is not the only jazz standard progression to use cycling dominants like this. Another famous example is found in the tune *Yesterdays* by Jerome Kern.

Yesterdays begins in the key of D Minor, but moves through several keys during its 16-bar progression.

Example 4o starts at bar seven of the song. It moves through a ii–V in the key of A Minor (Bm7b5 – E7) then, instead of resolving to an A minor chord, moves to A7. This begins a cycle that goes through six different dominant chords before eventually resolving to BbMaj7.

Example 4o:

In our Western system of music there are twelve notes and therefore twelve possible dominant chords. This progression from *Yesterdays* uses half of them!

Here's another bassline for this progression.

Example 4p:

This brings us to our final example in this chapter. It doesn't come from a jazz standard, but is a brilliant exercise to practice building basslines on these kinds of progressions. You've guessed it, we're going to cycle through all twelve dominant chords.

Example 4q:

Practice Tip

After you've played Example 4q, spend as much time as possible using the strategies we've discussed to come up with your own walking basslines on this sequence.

Just pick one strategy at a time (for example, adding a chromatic approach note on beats 2 and 4) and play for as long as you can. Then try another approach before combining them.

I've included a backing track for Example 4q for you to practice with.

Chapter Five – Static Chord Vamp

Playing a convincing jazz walking bassline on multiple bars of a single chord can be quite a challenge due to the limited note options available, but this is the challenge we'll address in this chapter.

A well-crafted walking bassline should have a sense of flow and movement, but this can seem difficult to achieve with static harmony. So, when the same chord extends over several bars, how do we keep the bassline from becoming repetitive?

Let's explore some strategies to create a feeling of movement even when the harmony remains unchanged.

Here are two examples of walking basslines played on just one Dm7 chord. I've focused on using chord tones to maintain interest and momentum.

Example 5a:

Example 5b:

Modal Jazz was a significant innovation in the late 1950s and came to people's attention with Miles Davis' landmark album, *Kind of Blue*. This style of jazz simplifies the musical structure by reducing the number of chord changes, and focuses on improvisation with scales or modes instead of traditional arpeggio ideas.

A standout track from *Kind of Blue* is *So What* – one of the rare jazz standards where the melody is primarily carried by the bass. The structure of *So What* consists of two eight-bar sections in an AABA form, similar to Rhythm Changes.

However, unlike Rhythm Changes, there are no chord changes *within* the sections. The A section is based entirely on a Dm7 chord, or more precisely, on the D Dorian scale.

Here are the notes that make up the D Dorian scale:

D Dorian

D	E	F	G	A	B	C
R	2nd	3rd	4th	5th	6th	7th

Example 5c uses only the notes from D Dorian to construct the bassline.

The strategy here is to place the chord tones of Dm7 (D F A C) on the strong 1 and 3 beats, then play any note from the scale on beats 2 and 4.

Example 5c:

Here's another example.

Example 5d:

Now I'm going to add more movement into the bassline by using a bigger melodic range. The lowest note in Example 5e is the open E, and the highest note is D on the 7th fret of the G string – a range of nearly two octaves.

This range allows the use of larger interval jumps. For instance, in bars one and seven of Example 5e, and bars five and seven of Example 5f, you'll notice intervals of more than an octave between consecutive notes. Each time, I use an open string to provide extra time to shift my fretting-hand position.

Example 5e:

Example 5f uses an even wider range, with the highest note being a 10th fret F. Here, the bassline spans over two octaves.

Example 5f:

While large interval jumps can sound challenging if played too often, if used sparingly, they create a sense of change and movement in the music.

Here's another example using the same approach. I've included a couple of larger interval jumps in bars five and seven that don't rely on open strings. In both instances, the intervals are formed by moving from a fretted note on the first string to a nearby fretted note on the fourth string. This technique allows us to play intervals of a 9th and 10th.

Example 5g:

A 10th is essentially a 3rd played up an octave. They are particularly beautiful and work well on the bass, so I recommend experimenting with them in your lines.

Now, let's add some chromatic notes as passing notes and approach notes.

Example 5h:

Example 5i:

To keep the bassline sounding like D Dorian, it's crucial to place the important chord tones on the strong beats. This ensures that the chromatic notes are heard only as passing tones. Placing them on the strong beats would sound like we'd altered the harmony.

Here's another example to illustrate this approach.

Example 5j:

Another effective strategy for modal basslines is to imagine you're playing chord changes within the mode.

When playing in D Dorian, you can think of the Dm7 as chord ii in the key of C Major. If we view the progression as ii–V instead of just ii, we can then introduce G7-based ideas in any even-numbered bar.

This works well because all the notes of the G7 chord (G B D F) are found in the D Dorian mode, allowing us to play these notes on the strong beats without straying from the key.

Example 5k:

Example 5l:

Example 5m:

The B section of *So What* modulates up a half-step to Ebm7, which has the chord tones Eb, Gb, Bb and Db. Again, we can use the Dorian mode to form our basslines.

Here are the notes of Eb Dorian.

Eb Dorian

Eb	F	Gb	Ab	Bb	C	Db
R	2nd	3rd	4th	5th	6th	7th

Example 5n:

Because Eb Dorian is a half-step above D Dorian, in theory we could shift all the D Dorian examples up one fret. However, it's not that simple! The main issue is that the notes on the open strings do not occur in Eb Dorian, so we need to use them differently.

In Example 5o, I've used the open strings as chromatic approach notes. The open A string acts as an approach note for the 5th (Bb) in bar three.

In bar four, I've used the open D string as a chromatic approach note, positioned a half step below the root (Eb).

Additionally, I've used the open E string as a chromatic approach note above the root towards the end of bar six. However, to maintain continuity, I've shifted the target note (Eb) up an octave at the beginning of bar seven, which allows me to shift my hand position up the neck and extend the range of my bassline to the higher frets.

Example 5o:

Here's another example.

Example 5p:

For another example of a minor modal jazz tune, check out *Impressions* by John Coltrane. It follows the same structure as *So What*, so you can apply the bassline ideas from *So What*. However, *Impressions* is played at a much faster tempo!

Practice Tip

It's a good idea to practice transposing basslines into different keys. When you do this, it might be tempting to avoid using the open strings and instead rely solely on moving fretted notes around, using the same patterns and fingerings in each key.

However, by doing so, you will miss out on the advantages that the open strings offer, such as making it easier to navigate the neck and shift positions quickly. Remember that you can use an open string as a chord tone *or* a passing note, so don't hesitate to incorporate open strings into your basslines in any key.

Chapter Six – Playing Over a Jazz Blues

Now we've explored how to outline the major chord progressions in jazz, we're ready to move onto longer sequences. The major and minor ii–V–Is, the I–VI–ii–V sequence, and static chord vamps are all fundamental building blocks in jazz harmony, and mastering them will equip you for playing over hundreds of standard tunes. In chapters six and seven we'll put that knowledge to the test by first playing over a jazz-blues progression, and then the chord changes to one of the most famous jazz standards.

First up, let's explore the twelve-bar blues progression – a staple in jazz and the most common chord progression in the genre. We'll start by looking at how to craft a walking bassline through a complete chorus of a twelve-bar blues in Bb.

While there are many variations to a twelve-bar blues, a basic version might typically involve just three chords: Bb7, Eb7 and F7.

In Chapter Three, we discovered that in the key of Bb Major, chords I, IV and V are BbMaj7, EbMaj7 and F7. However, in the blues, the I and IV chords are also played as dominant chords (Bb7 and Eb7) by flattening the 7th of each. Bb7 includes an Ab instead of an A, and Eb7 has a Db instead of a D.

Example 6a shows a straightforward three-chord blues progression. Despite its simplicity, this progression offers ample opportunity to craft a compelling jazz bassline by using chord tones and the passing note patterns we explored earlier.

Example 6a:

In Example 6b, note how I've placed chord tones other than the root on certain chord changes to create inversions. In bar two, I play a G, which is the 3rd of the Eb7 chord, and in bar five, I play a Db (the b7). I also used the b7 at the start of bar seven, playing an Ab on the Bb7 chord.

Example 6b:

In Example 6c, we extend the range of the bassline all the way up to the 15th fret (Bb) on the first string. This shows you how you can effectively expand the melodic range of your line in a standard blues structure.

This line works its way up the fretboard then, having gone beyond the 12th fret, we can use an open string to navigate our way back into the bass register.

In bar four, a large interval jump is created by using the open D string after the Bb on the 15th fret of the G string. The D functions as both a chord tone and a chromatic approach note to the root of the Eb7 chord on beat one.

Example 6c:

It can sound nice to venture into the higher register as long as we don't stay there too long.

Examples 6a, 6b and 6c showed how to play a jazz walking bassline on a three-chord blues. However, in jazz, the twelve-bar blues normally contains a lot more chords. Jazz musicians will often add many of the chord progressions we've looked at in this book.

In a jazz blues, the change to chord IV is usually preceded by a ii–V in the previous bar.

In bar eight, the chord progression will usually either go to chord VI (G7), or to chord iii (Dm7) then chord VI, which is how I've written it in Example 6d. This is the start of a Cycle of 5ths sequence: iii–VI–ii–V. Once that's resolved to the I chord there's a I–VI–ii–V turnaround to take us back to the top of the progression.

Here's one way to play a bassline over this sequence.

Example 6d:

Here's another way to approach the changes.

Example 6e:

In the following examples I've extended the range into more positions on the neck.

Example 6f:

Example 6g

Cm7   **F7**   **B♭7**   **G7**   **Cm7**   **F7**

Bb is a popular key for jazz because it's a good key for horn players. F is another popular key because it works well for both horns and piano. To help prepare you for more musical situations, the next examples use the same chord changes transposed to the key of F.

In Example 6h, the bassline stays in the lower positions on the neck.

Example 6h:

F7   **B♭7**   **F7**   **Cm7**   **F7**

B♭7   **Bdim7**   **F7**   **Am7**   **D7**

Gm7   **C7**   **F7**   **D7**   **Gm7**   **C7**

In the following examples I've increased the range into higher positions.

Example 6i:

This idea introduces some larger interval jumps.

In bar three there is a large jump from the open A up to an Eb at the 8th fret. There's also a descending interval of two octaves in bar ten. Finally, in the last bar I've used an ascending minor 10th followed by a large descending interval from C to E on the open string.

Example 6j:

There are an abundance of free jazz-blues backing tracks available online, so practice your walking lines on the jazz-blues in lots of different keys. Keep your focus on targeting the chord tones and using approach notes, and try to avoid falling into repetitive patterns.

Chapter Seven – Playing Over a Jazz Standard

In this chapter, we're going to explore the chord changes of the well-known jazz standard *All the Things You Are* by Jerome Kern. It's usually played in the key of Ab Major, and the first eight bars introduce a Cycle of 5ths progression before modulating to C Major.

Example 7a:

The chords in this key are:

Ab	Bb	C	Db	Eb	F	G
I	ii	iii	IV	V	vi	vii
AbMaj7	Bbm7	Cm7	DbMaj7	Eb7	Fm7	Gm7b5
Ab C Eb G	Bb Db F Ab	C Eb G Bb	Db F Ab C	Eb G Bb Db	F Ab C Eb	G Bb Db F

In bars 2-4 we can see a ii–V–I sequence. However, the Cycle of 5ths progression extends beyond this basic ii–V–I. It begins with chord vi (Fm7) which is a 5th away from chord ii. Following the I chord, the cycle continues into the next bar with chord IV (DbMaj7).

This means that the complete cycle is vi–ii–V–I–IV in Ab Major, followed by a ii–V–I in C Major.

Example 7b, contains several different strategies.

In bar one, a descending sequence moves chromatically from the root note of the first chord (Fm7) to the 3rd of Bbm7.

The line continues its descent in bar two, using scale notes as passing tones, then resolves to the 3rd of the Eb7 chord at the start of bar three.

In bars 3-4, the range is extended with some slightly larger intervals that mainly target chord tones.

In bar four, the open G string (the 7th of AbMaj7) allows a shift to the 8th fret where I play Eb (the 5th).

Bars five and six contain an arpeggio pattern starting from the root of the DbMaj7 chord that descends to the 3rd. It then ascends from the 3rd to the 5th and then the 7th.

This pattern repeats on the next chord (Dm7) but when the chord changes to G7, I target the root and 3rd of G7 instead of continuing to the 5th and 7th of the Dm7.

After the root of the CMaj7 chord in bar seven, there's a large interval jump to the 3rd that's played on the open E string. Use the open string to shift your hand position once again.

Example 7b:

Example 7c:

In the next eight-bar section, the sequence repeats, but is played in two new keys, Eb Major, and G Major.

Example 7d:

In bar six of Example 7e, the two open strings are the root notes of the Am7 and D7 chords and are once again an opportunity to shift position with my left hand.

Contrast these open string root notes to how the open strings in the first four bars were all passing notes.

Example 7e:

This example starts in a higher position and descends.

Example 7f:

Now let's move into the middle-eight section.

It begins with a ii–V–I progression in G Major, the same key that closed the previous section. Then, there's another ii–V–I progression that seems to lead towards E Minor, but an E Major chord is played to subvert the listener's expectation.

The C7 chord at the end guides us back into another A section in the original key.

Example 7g:

You should be getting quite familiar with walking on ii–V–I progressions by now, so let's increase the range from the low E string up to the 12th fret of the G string.

I've added the open strings both as chord tones and passing notes, using them to facilitate movement across the fretboard and shift positions. Additionally, I played some 10th intervals in bars four, seven, and eight.

Example 7h:

Here's another route through these changes.

Example 7i:

All the Things You Are follows an AABA structure, although each A section is played in a different key.

The final A section begins similarly to the first, but instead of shifting to a new key (C Major) it contains an extended sequence that resolves back to the original key of Ab Major.

This final section follows the chords of the first section for the first five bars: vi–ii–V–I–IV. But there's a change in bar seven. The root note from the IV chord remains, but the chord changes from DbMaj7 to Dbm7. We can think of this as a minor IV chord.

Note: Using a minor chord IV in a major key is quite common in jazz and other styles of music. The Beatles used it in the song *Blackbird*, and another jazz standard featuring the same idea is *All of Me*.

In bar seven the chord drops a half step to Cm7, which is chord iii. The following chord is B diminished, and the root notes continue to descend in half steps to Bbm7 in bar nine. Bbm7 is now chord ii, and the progression ends with a ii–V–I.

The final bar is a minor ii–V, which leads us back to the Fm7 chord at the beginning of the first section.

The chord tones for Bdim7 are B, D, F and Ab. These are the notes that I've used in bar eight of the following two examples.

Example 7j:

Example 7k:

Here's one final example.

Example 7l:

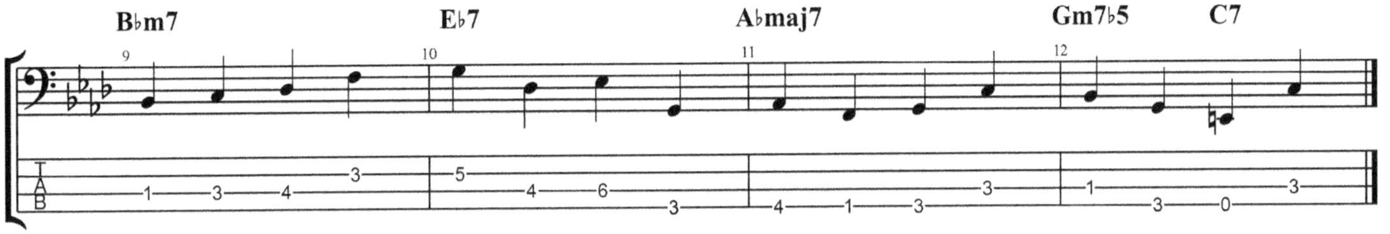
B♭m7
E♭7
A♭maj7
Gm7♭5
C7
9
10
11
12
T
A
B

Conclusion

To master walking basslines that effectively outline the harmony of a jazz tune, it's crucial to familiarize yourself with the common chord sequences found in many jazz standards. The aim of this book has been to equip you with strategies to navigate these sequences with confidence.

Understanding chord tones (arpeggios) is fundamental to playing jazz on the bass, but recognizing key changes, scale degrees, and the relationship of chords within a key are equally important.

Remember the two simple guidelines that will help you to articulate the harmony in any jazz chord sequence:

1. Place the chord tones on beats 1 and 3.

2. Use passing notes on beats 2 and 4 to connect the chord tones.

However, you should approach these rules with flexibility. Jazz is an improvised music and not about adhering strictly to rules.

Understanding harmony means knowing the chord progression in your head and crafting a bassline that complements it well. If you find that deviating from these rules or applying different ones helps capture the essence of the progression, then by all means embrace that creativity.

To truly grasp what makes a great walking bassline, listening widely is key. When learning a new jazz standard, immerse yourself in different renditions of it by various artists to gain a broader perspective before attempting to play it yourself. Start with the standards mentioned in this book and expand from there.

Remember, crafting a great bassline is not solely about the notes you choose – your timing and tone are just as critical. Practicing with a metronome set to click on beats 2 and 4 at a comfortable tempo will help to develop your rhythmic accuracy. Aim for each note to resonate clearly and maintain relaxation to ensure a smooth flow in your playing.

Additionally, great tone isn't just about your instrument's hardware, it starts with your technique. For a rounder, more authentic jazz sound, try plucking the strings nearer to the fretboard rather than the bridge, and keep your touch light.

Finally, don't hesitate to experiment to find your own voice. Every renowned jazz bassist has carved out their own unique sound and approach. While you're exploring, focus on making discerning note choices, developing a solid feel for time, and refining your tone.

Above all, have fun with it.

Johnny.

By The Same Author

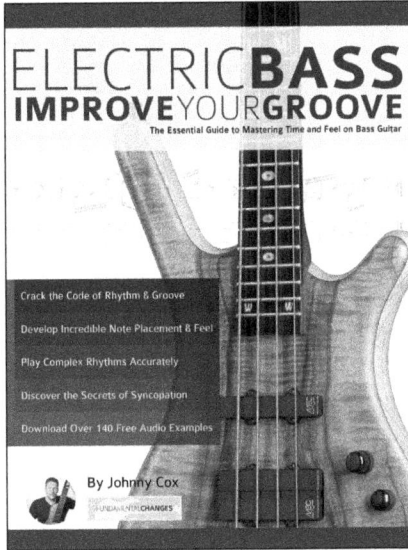

Crack the Code of Rhythm, Groove and Feel on Electric Bass Guitar

• Discover how to groove flawlessly on bass in any style of music

• Master bass guitar rhythm and placement

• Play in the pocket, every time.

Build your groove and play bass like a master

• Discover how to groove flawlessly on electric bass in any style of music

• Understand bass guitar rhythm and placement

• Play in the pocket, every time.

Every bass player wants to play with groove and great feel. These skills are what tie a performance together, move the music forward, and keep it "in the pocket". Groove is what your audience wants to hear. **Electric Bass – Improve Your Groove** is a complete course in rhythm and groove on bass. Groove is built by understanding rhythm, playing accurately and sharing that feel with other musicians.

What you'll learn:

• How to play in time on bass guitar

• How to play "in the pocket" to create a tight, grooving performance

• How to crack the code of rhythm and groove

• The secrets of syncopation and building your internal clock

• The Konnakol vocal counting system to help you groove without thinking

• 5 complete pieces with backing tracks that put theory into practice

• Over 140 exercises and examples with FREE supporting audio to download

Building perfect time and feel on bass is explained from absolute basics to teach you how to play basslines with great rhythm, from the simplest to the most complex grooves.

You'll discover grooving bass guitar rhythms and develop devastating accuracy and feel. Rock, Funk, Jazz, Blues and Latin feels on bass are all intimately addressed with over 140 examples and backing tracks.